ISBN-13:978-1547269167
ISBN-10:1547269162

www.cyprusstrays.com

CYPRUS DOG TAILS

Real Stray Dog Stories From The Voices Of The Animals

Natalie Reed

ISBN-13:978-1547269167
ISBN-10:1547269162

www.cyprusstrays.com

DEDICATION

This book is dedicated to my husband Mark, without him none of these gorgeous dogs would have stood a chance. This book is also dedicated to all those animal lovers around the world who endeavor to help stray and unwanted animals to find their forever homes.

CONTENTS

ACKNOWLEDGMENTS

THANKS TO REVEKKA DIMITRIOU FOR HER FANTASTIC DESIGN WORK
WITH THIS BOOK.

DISCLAIMER
ALL THE STORIES IN THIS BOOK ARE TRUE ACCOUNTS, HOWEVER
SOME SPECULATION HAS BEEN MADE AS TO THE LIVES OF THESE
DOGS BEFORE THEY WERE RESCUED.

EVERY ATTEMPT WAS MADE TO FIND THE ORIGINAL OWNERS OF
THESE DOGS
NONE OF WHICH CAME FORWARD.

Help Us Help More Strays!

All proceeds from this book will go towards securing the land that all the gorgeous dogs in this book currently enjoy the benefit of. Once the land is secured we can help more strays and foster more dogs until we can help find them a forever home.

If you have enjoyed this book and want to help please recommend others to buy it for themselves and to therefore contribute to this fantastic cause.

You can also visit our website **www.cyprusstrays.com** where you can register for our monthly 'pupdates' about all the dogs in this book and hopefully the many more we will be able to help in the future.

Thank you for caring.... *Natalie*

Chapter 1

SHAMMY - NUMBER ONE

I was the first, it was me that started all this! Let me tell you how it all began.

As a new born pup I was taken on by a family who seemed to love and adore me. As I grew a little bigger, I have to admit I got very excited, a lot! I wouldn't walk properly on a lead, I just couldn't concentrate for long enough, I had to jump up and down all the time because I was so excited. I also liked to nip people's ankles, I wasn't trying to be rough I just wanted everyone to go in the direction I wanted them to go in and nipping their ankles with my little puppy teeth seemed to do the trick... well it certainly made them jump into action!

One day my family, who had seemed to be getting mad at me quite a lot lately, told me to jump in the car as we were going on an adventure. I was so excited I jumped straight in, not noticing they had also brought my bowl with us...mmm strange.

We got to a village area and drove down a Farmers lane. It was pretty dark and there was nobody about but I was so excited about my adventure I didn't really notice at the time. They opened the boot and encouraged me to jump out. They didn't even try to put my lead on me. Finally I thought, they must have learnt that I am better without a lead!

Before I knew it they had placed my bowl in the field with some biscuits in it and jumped back in the car and drove off. I was so busy running and diving in the field I didn't notice at first but when I turned back to see them and show them how high I could jump over the long grass, they had gone and I was all alone! Suddenly I felt scared. I had no clue where I was, it was getting really dark and although I have a big fluffy, curly coat I suddenly felt cold and alone.

After a couple of hours of waiting for my family to return, I could see a light in the distance as a car was pulling up into a driveway. It seemed so far away but I thought it might be them coming back for me so I ran as fast as I could towards them.

As I got closer, I realised it wasn't them, the car was a different colour and two men and a lady got out. I slowed down a little, I wasn't sure if I should get closer but I was lost and scared and it was the first people I had seen since I had been left on my own.

As I got closer the man who was driving spotted me. He bent down and started calling out to me nice and softly. Slowly I approached him and he stroked me and started talking to me. I felt so relieved. Next thing I knew he had disappeared into the house. I thought he had left me but soon enough he came back outside with what was the most delicious sausage I had ever tasted and I was really, really hungry by this time. Soon another car pulled up. Could this be my family coming back for me? No, it was a lady who pulled up on the same drive. As soon as she saw me she gave me a big stroke and a cuddle, I felt so happy… sausages and cuddles!

I heard the man who gave me the sausage say he was worried I was a stray but the lady thought I was just wandering around and that I must belong to someone as I had a blue collar on and that they should leave me to go home to my family. They gave me one final stroke and another sausage, then left me and went to bed leaving me alone once more outside their house.

All of a sudden it started to rain, so I ran under their car port to get some shelter but then I started to worry that if they came back outside they wouldn't know I was there and would think I had found my family and there would be no more sausages or cuddles so I sat outside their front door in the pouring rain until the morning, dreaming of more tasty sausages and loving cuddles.

The next morning, the man who gave me the sausages the night before came to the door with the lady. They opened the door and the lady was panicking when she saw how wet I was, I didn't care I was just so happy to see them. They took me inside their house, found a towel and dried me off and then… yes you guessed it, they gave me another sausage! Just then the other lady and the man I had seen in the car the night before came downstairs. They both ran up to me and cuddled me as well. I was in doggy heaven!

I heard the first lady saying that they couldn't keep me as I probably belonged to someone. The man who gave me the sausages spoke to the other man and they told the lady they were going to take me to the local vets to see if I was 'chipped' to see if I belonged to anyone. They got a piece of rope and tied it to my collar and guided me out to the car. I really tried to be good on the lead as I wanted them to like me and didn't want to get in trouble.

After a trip to the vets which confirmed I wasn't 'chipped' the two men left me in the car whilst they went into a shop. They came back with bags full of things. I wondered if it might be bags full of sausages. I so hoped it was and that they weren't going to drop me in a field somewhere like my family had. I was so happy when we pulled up back at their house a short while afterwards.

'Sausage Man' as I now referred to him, removed my rope lead and pulled out a shiny new collar and lead from one of the bags from the shop. He then led me gently back into the house where the two ladies were waiting.

Out of the bags came even more treats. A dog bowl (I assumed for all the sausages), a ball and a tug toy. Whilst I sniffed into the shopping bags looking for sausages the two men went back to the car and pulled out a big dog house they called a kennel. I heard the man ask the lady whether they should keep me. She agreed that now they knew I wasn't tagged and no-one was looking for me that they would.

I was so excited I ran around the house four times non stop barking with delight. The man decided, as he was a car valeter, that he would call me Shammy after one of the cloths he used to clean the cars because of my big, thick black fluffy fur. I liked it and responded by giving him my paw, a trick I had learned when very young to try and impress my family and make sure they loved me and were not mad at me. Him and the lady gave me a great big cuddle.

So there it is, the story of how I met my Mummy and Daddy and found my loving, forever home. I am number One because I was the first. But that was just the beginning……..

Chapter 2

HENRY - TWO'S COMPANY

I have always hated being a gun dog from my first ever memories of it. Being locked up for most of every year in a cage with several other dogs and not having seen love, affection or in most cases even acknowledgement means life for a hunting dog isn't that great. Then of course comes the hunting itself, the one time you are actually let out of your cage. The first time you are so excited to experience so many different smells and places to dig and to feel the sun on your back and the wind in your big floppy ears and where you can run, run as fast as you can, free at last! I got so excited for that moment but after the first time it just filled me with dread.

The first time it happened we were let out of the cage and put into cages in a pickup truck. We drove for a short while and then our owner opened the cages and we were in a field which seemed to be in the middle of nowhere. I was so excited I nearly wet myself as I had never seen such beautiful grass and trees and couldn't wait to run free and have a good sniff around.

Like all the other dogs I stayed close to my owner for fear of getting into trouble, but I couldn't resist putting my nose to the ground and smelling the soil and the grass and then the fresh air. I will never forget this moment, it was the happiest I had ever been in my short doggie life up to that point. As I started to get brave and wander a bit further away to investigate a nearby bush I heard the loudest bang I have ever heard in my life. I was petrified and without thinking I ran, ran like the wind to a group of trees not far away and hid and cowered whilst the big loud bangs continued. I was so afraid, I didn't know what to do, I just froze.

I stayed behind the trees shivering for what seemed like forever when all of a sudden I felt a hand grab me by the scruff of my neck and drag me back to the truck. I was thrown in the truck and left there on my own whilst the loud bangs continued for several hours. I have never been so frightened in my life and couldn't understand what I had done wrong or why my owner had been so mad at me and called me useless or why the other dogs were still out there and I wasn't. Would the loud bangs ever stop? Would any of them ever come back?

They did eventually come back and when the other dogs got back in the truck they all made fun of me for being so scared. They had been allowed to run free and fetch dead birds that our owner had shot with his big loud banging stick. I envied the fact that they could run free but could not get over the loud bangs. My big floppy ears are so sensitive and the ringing in them from the bangs stayed with me for weeks, I would even have nightmares about it.

One day, I heard the horrible jangle of the keys to the cage, I knew that meant we were going hunting again. Since that first time it had pretty much been the same story. The bangs would start; I would be scared and be thrown back into the truck. This time the same thing happened but instead of getting thrown back into the truck I was tied with a piece of rope to the side of the truck making me even closer to the big banging stick and even more frightened than ever. Of course, my instinct was to run as far away from the bangs as possible and I pulled and pulled on the rope to break free but it was impossible. My owner moved further away into the distance and then turned and was firing his banging stick towards birds near me.

A stray bullet landed a couple of meters from me and I was so frightened I bolted as hard and as fast as I could and to my surprise the end of the rope tied to the truck broke free. I didn't stop to think about it I just ran and ran and ran. Eventually, when I couldn't hear the bangs anymore I flopped down in some long grass to catch my breath. I was really hot and very thirsty but there was no-one in sight and I couldn't even remember the way back to the truck or to my cage at the farm where we lived so I found some shelter under a tree and fell asleep.

The next morning, I woke up really hot and thirsty and although I was free to run and sniff and play I couldn't find the energy. All I could think about was food, shade and water. I decided I would search for water. So, I started walking through the fields searching for some sign of life or some water. After a good hour of walking I saw a big building in the distance, it was stood on its own in a field with lots of cars outside. I could also hear voices. I made my way as fast as I could which wasn't very fast as I was exhausted and the sun was very, very hot now. I saw a man outside the building cleaning some cars. I got as close to him as I could and as soon as he spotted me I just flopped to the ground I was so tired hot and thirsty and had come over all dizzy.

The man came over to me and gently stroked me. I was so relieved and had never had any human touch me in this way or show me so much kindness. He suddenly got up and went to a van nearby and came back with a big bottle of water. He held the bottle up for me and I opened my mouth and lapped it up as fast as I could I was so thirsty. After I had drunk the whole bottle of water, the man grabbed the rope that was still attached to me from the truck and led me into his van. It was lovely and cool and shaded in there and he pulled out a big rag for me to lay on. I was happy to go wherever he took me, he had shown me more kindness in ten minutes than any other human in my whole life. He grabbed some tools and put them in the van near me then shut all the doors, got in and started to drive. I didn't know where he was taking me but I didn't care, I just closed my eyes and fell asleep.

Henry

After about 20 minutes the van stopped and the back door opened, there was the man and there was also a lady looking in. The man grabbed the rope and calmly led me out of the van. The lady bent down and cuddled me straight away. I was a bit shocked at first as no-one had ever done that before but I really liked it and licked her face to show how grateful I was. They led me into the house and the lady prepared me a big bowl of meat and biscuits and a fresh bowl of water. I woofed down the food and water. I was so hungry and hadn't eaten for nearly two days.

After I had finished eating the lady removed my rope and called me to come outside with her. There in front of me stood a big black fluffy puppy. As soon as he saw me he ran straight up to me and started sniffing all round me and then started to gently nip my feet and body to try and get me to play. I had never played with the other dogs in the cage at the farm. We did not have much room in the cage and most of the time we were tired and hot and sad. I didn't respond at first but he was persistent and soon enough I felt happy and free and wanted to play back. We ran around the big garden a few times and playfully nipped each other. The lady came up to me and gave me another big cuddle and told me that I was very handsome and looked like a true gentleman so I would be called Henry. I liked the name and licked her face again to show my approval. The rest of the day I spent playing with the big fluffy puppy who I now know is called Shammy. He even let me share his tug toy and kennel.

The next day the lady took me to see the nice vet. He checked me over and said I was healthy but very lucky that the man had found me when he did as I would not have survived the heat and dehydration for much longer. A simple check showed that I was not chipped which meant I did not belong to anyone. I was so relieved that I did not have to go back to the farm, the cage and the loud banging stick.

I settled in with my new family straight away and loved having a play mate. Regular food, walks and cuddles were now my daily routine, I was in doggy heaven. Some nights there would be big flashes of light and bangs from the sky and I would shiver and cower remembering my days as a hunting dog but then I would cuddle up to my big furry friend Shammy and remember I had nothing to fear as I was now in my forever home, protected and loved.

Chapter 3

LUCKY NUMBER THREE

I remember being a happy playful puppy. I had four brothers and sisters who looked like me but some were brown and some were black and brown or black and white. I however, was the only pure white puppy of the litter.

When I was just a few weeks old a family with children came to visit. Our mummy told us we were a very special breed and that people would come to see us and choose us to go and live in a special home with them. I was sad to know I would be leaving my mother so soon but she reassured me that to be picked was a great compliment and that I would go to live with a family who I would love and protect for the rest of my life in return for food, walks and affection.

After this chat with my mummy I felt very excited and wanted to be picked. My mummy had told me that because I was the only one of all my brothers and sisters that was pure white that I was very special. This made me even more confident that the first visiting family would choose me.

I don't know if it was how I kept jumping in front of my brothers and sister and trying to do tricks or my big puppy smile but sure enough the first family arrived and picked me. I was so excited about my new life but sad to be leaving my mummy and brothers and sisters even though most of the time my brothers annoyed me and tried to pick on me because I was a girl and the only pure white of the family. I gave my mummy a big hug goodbye and bit my brothers affectionately. I licked my sister and then one of the children from the family scooped me up, sat me on her knee in the car and I was off to start my new exciting life with my new family. I knew I would love and protect them forever just as mummy had told me to.

The first few weeks of my life with my new family were fantastic. The little girl would cuddle me and play with me and even put little flowers behind my ears and a necklace around my neck. I didn't mind, I loved all the attention. I would sleep outside in my kennel and the boy from the family would take me for a walk every day. He also taught me to sit on command and how to walk on a lead. At night if anyone walked past the house or came near the gate I would put on my scariest voice and growl and bark to let strangers know I was there to protect my family, my mummy would be so proud.

One day I was playing with the little girl in the garden and she screamed out to her mummy. Her mummy ran outside and came to see what all the fuss was about. The little girl was pointing to my head and parts of my back. I couldn't understand what was going on but the mummy said that I was faulty as I had scabs all over me and if they didn't clear up soon they would take me back. I was so upset. I have always been proud of being the only pure white dog of the litter yet something was happening to my skin and my new family didn't like it.

The little girl stopped playing with me and the little boy stopped taking me for walks. I tried my best to lick my scabs better but that seemed to make them worse. I still guarded the garden barking and growling at any passer-by to prove to my family that I could still do my job and to remind them that I was still here. But now all they seemed to do was get mad at me for barking, in fact they were mad at me for everything. No more walks or cuddles, no more praise or appreciation, I spent most of my time feeling alone and unwanted and all the time my scabs were getting worse.

One day the family went out and left the gate open. They had always been so careful before to shut it so I wouldn't leave the garden. They were gone for hours and I had become so lonely I couldn't resist leaving the garden to go and explore a nearby field and the dog that lived at the other side of it, I just wanted someone to play with as I was still just a puppy. I walked up to the house at the other side of the field playfully excited about meeting a new friend. When I got to the gate I realised the dog was very big, loud and scary. He was attached to a long chain and came bounding to the gate shouting and barking at me, he was so big and so aggressive and so loud and I didn't know if his chain would stop him from getting to me. He could have eaten me in one go, his teeth were that big and sharp. Frightened for my life I ran and ran, narrowly missed by a speeding car as I fled for my life along a busy main road.

By this time, I was totally lost and in a built-up area where there were lots of shops and restaurants. I felt sure that once my family got back and realised I had gone missing they would come and look for me. Several hours passed as I walked down the road. There were people everywhere. I saw a family that looked just like mine up ahead in the distance. They had obviously come to take me home and maybe start to love me again. They started to walk down a sloping road towards the sea, I ran as fast I could to catch up with them dodging people's feet and cars as I crossed the road. I just got within a couple of meters from them when they walked into a building with big glass doors that opened as they approached. I ran to catch up before the doors closed but just as I got there the doors closed on me and I banged my nose as I tried to run through them. Picking myself up I stared through the glass doors willing my family to turn around and see me. Just as they were walking away the little girl from the family turned around and to my dismay it was not my family.

With a heavy head, I started to walk back up the slope towards the main road. I had no idea how to get home and I was tired and hungry. It had suddenly got very dark and the road was full of people and very noisy. As I was still very small I had to try and jump out of the way of people's feet so as not to get trodden on. I don't know where I was but I had never seen so many people walking up and down a street or heard so much loud music and seen so many flashing lights.

I decided I needed to get away from here so I ran down a side street. There was a big shop and at the back of it were two big bins that were overflowing. I could smell something coming from the bin, something that smelled like food. I was hungry and so I rummaged through the bags on the floor at the bottom of the bin and managed to find some bread and a tiny bit of what I think was chicken. By this time, I was tired and famished and I was grateful for anything to eat. I knew there was no-way I could find my way home now it was dark so I curled up into the smallest ball I possibly could underneath the bin and eventually fell to sleep.

The next morning, I was awoken by a man shouting at me. He was shooing me away from under the bins and waving his arm. I had only just woken up and was tired and confused but he started to shout louder and become more aggressive so I soon got to my feet and ran. After running for quite a while I stopped to catch my breath. I was full of sadness at being lost and alone but also because I longed to have my family back to the way it was before I got my stupid scabs. I licked my sores which had become really itchy and longed to be the beautiful pure white girl in the litter I once was before. I thought about my mummy and what she might say to me now that I had failed my family, I felt terrible and wondered if I would ever be my happy playful self again.

I was interrupted from my thoughts by the smell of meat, freshly cooked delicious meat. I lifted my nose to the air and followed the smell up onto the busy road where I had been the night before. The smell was coming from a restaurant with people sat outside. I decided I would put my cutest puppy face on and a big smile and see if I could get something to eat. As I approached the restaurant a lady sat outside saw me. I heard her mention to the man she was sat nek to how cute I was and should they give me some of their meat. Well once I heard this I went into super cute mode rubbing up against her legs and attempting my cutest puppy smile ever. She bent down and stroked me and gave me a big lump of what was the most delicious freshly cooked meat I had ever tasted. Yummy. I was just about to give her another cute puppy look as the meat was so nice when a man with a big bellowing voice came to the front of the restaurant shouting at me to go away. I looked up at the lady who had fed me to help but she turned back to the table as the man swiftly kicked me with the end of his shoe, not so hard that he broke any bones but hard enough to scare me as he was so big and I was so small.

Lucky

Just then a lady and a man I had never seen before ran up behind me and scooped me up. The lady cuddled me into her chest and was saying sweet loving things to me. She carried me for a while then gave me to the man who got into a car and sat me on his knee. He was really nice and so I snuggled into his chest whilst the lady drove the car.

Soon after this we arrived to see a nice man who was a vet called Tasos. He checked me and said I had ear lice but he could give the lady some medicine to fix me and he also said that my scabs which were really itchy especially in the sun could be helped with some special injections and that they would mostly clear up with no problem. He gave the lady all he medicine and checked to see if I was tagged but I wasn't. I was upset that my family hadn't registered me as their dog but remembering the last few weeks of my life there and then my short time on the streets I was just glad someone cared. The lady and the man took me to the lady's house. The man left and the lady gave me some yummy meat and biscuits which I was so grateful for and a big drink of water and then she sat and cuddled me. Finally, someone loved and wanted me again.

Shortly afterwards another man arrived at the house, I was a little frightened in case he would not love me like the lady did. He said he might have a friend that was looking for a dog like me to have in their home but I had been through so much and I felt so safe I didn't want to leave. The lady took me outside and made a special place for me, with shade and a bed and some biscuits and water. I was so excited I knocked the biscuits all over the floor. This made me scared that her or the man would be mad at me for this and I cowered in the corner. But they were not mad they just cuddled me and scooped up the biscuits and said it didn't matter.

Through the fence where they had made my bed I could see two boy dogs. One big black fluffy one that kept yapping and one brown handsome one who was quiet but kept trying to sniff me with his big wet nose through the fence. They were both much bigger than me but I wasn't scared I wanted to play with them. I spent the night feeling safe but was scared about where I would be going or who would be taking me in the morning.

The next morning, I woke to the sound of the lady opening the gate and bringing me more yummy food and biscuits. She had seen me sniffing and licking the two boy dogs through the fence so one at a time let them in to meet me. I hadn't played with any other dogs since I left my brothers and sisters several months ago and I was excited and not scared one bit.

Both boys were very friendly and I was so happy to be playing and have some company. Just then the man came back and said that his friend was interested in having me but the lady said no and that I had been through enough and that I was settled there now and that she thought I should stay. I ran up to the man and started licking him and making a fuss of him. I really wanted to stay and thought if I could just make him love me too then this would be my perfect home with a perfect family.

The man started to stroke me and then took me in with the two other dogs together who I now know to be Shammy and Henry. We had fun together and they were very nice to me. We all sniffed each other for a while then started to run around and play it was so much fun. Shammy kept nipping at my ankles to try and get me to go in a certain direction but I didn't mind, it reminded me of my brothers I had left behind. The man came up to me and stroked me again and said that I was a very lucky girl and that I could stay. I was so excited and I think Henry and Shammy were too as we all ran around the garden and licked the man and the woman to express our thanks.

So, the man who I now know as Daddy named me Lucky. I am a lot bigger now, bigger than my two brothers but I will never forget my journey to find my forever home and how lucky I really was.

Chapter 4

MUSIC FOR MOLLY

My young puppy days were so traumatic for me that I have blocked most of it out.

I had been roaming the streets for a very long time and I have always been very wary of people as what I do remember is humans are cruel and scary and violent. Because I had been badly treated in the past when people in local shops and bars tried to help me I always ran away trying to protect myself and prevent getting hurt again.

Of course, I was very hungry and so when the people left me food out in a bowl I waited until they were out of sight and grabbed something to eat. I could feel my body getting thinner and thinner and it sure beat having to scrounge for food in dustbins or fight off other stray cats and dogs to enable me to eat.

I have had a limp for as long as I can remember, I am not sure why or how I injured myself but I managed ok to get around. One day I was running across the road to see if I could find something to eat when a big car came whizzing and before I knew it, I felt my feet taken from beneath me and was laid unable to move in the middle of the road whilst the driver did not even care and just drove off & left me for dead!

The local people I had been so scared of came to the road to help me. I could not run away as I could not move! They took me to a local vet called Medvets who gave me x-rays and told the people if no-one could pay for me to get better I would go to the pound and eventually have to be put down. To be honest I had felt so scared, sad, lonely and lost for such a long time that even I began to think it might be for the best.

However, the local people would not be deterred and they had been rallying around to try and help raise money for me to get better. I started eating a little more every day and the vet told me that I had been offered a loving forever home with a family who have three other dogs who were once scared and abandoned just like me.

The next day my new mummy came to see me for the first time. She said I looked like a Molly, I wasn't sure what she meant by this at the time but over time realised that that was the name she had given me and to be honest I really like it, it suits me. I was a bit wary of her at first as I didn't really like people as they scared me but she soothed me and tickled my belly and told me about my new home and my two new brothers and my new sister I would be going to live with. I heard her talking to the vet who said my pelvis was healing well but I may need more than one operation and I could be in the doggy hospital for some time! I found it really hard to move around too much as I was in a lot of pain although the nice lady 'Natalie' at the vets gave me some pain killers to help. I had some x-rays... that was scary but they said I had to have them so they could see how to make me better. Although I was still scared I secretly hoped my new mummy would come back the next day to see me as I was getting used to her voice and her smell and it was the first time in my life I had experienced belly tickles which to my surprise I really liked.

As the days passed I spent more and more time with my new mummy who visited me in the doggy hospital every day. Every time I saw her I became less and less scared for my future. She always told me stories about the place where I was going to live, where there would be lots of space for me to run around and hardly a car or road in sight. I was secretly getting excited although before this I have been excited but things have never worked out and I always ended up hungry and alone. I hoped that this time it would be different!

One day I heard my new Mummy talking to the vet who said it would cost up to €1200 to get me fit and well again as I needed one or even two operations plus I needed to be cared for and needed special medicine. That sounded like a lot, I hoped that all the people mummy had asked to try and help raise the money for me would think I was worth it and will help me. I so wanted to be able to run and play again especially now that I had a new home to look forward to and brothers and a sister waiting for me.

One day not so long after that I met my new Daddy for the first time. His voice was a lot deeper than mummy's and I didn't know his smell so I was a bit frightened but he did stroke me and talk nicely to me. I was excited to see my mummy, I even cocked my leg a little so she would tickle my belly... I loved a belly tickle.....in fact I still do.

The vet said I was healing so well that I may not need the operation on my pelvis. Just one on my hip. I remember thinking that this was good news and it meant that all being well I would be able to go to my forever home soon and meet my new brothers and sister.

My mummy came to see me every day except for nasty Bank Holidays which I didn't like because mummy did not come, although the vet reassured me that there wouldn't be too many more Bank Holiday's before I went to my forever home. Every time Mummy came to see me she fed me yummy biscuits. The nice lady from the vets, who was also called Natalie, would bring them out so mummy could feed me. I was still really shy with mummy but the hungrier I was the less shy I got. I had made progress though and I was now walking around my cage more but was still scared to come out of it and walk around as I had got so used to being safe and protected in there.

Mummy said it was nearly time for me to go to my new home so when I was alone in the day I would sit and think about what it would be like. Would I like my new brothers and sister? Would they like me? Would I be able to run again like I used to do before my accident? Would my mummy and daddy love me forever and ever? I really hoped so. My mummy told me my new home has so much space to run around in and that my new brothers and sister would help me to get back on my feet again. I was so very excited to have other doggies to play with...I was just worried I would have to share my dinner with them!

The day came when mummy told me that through the efforts of lots of local people and her and the guitarist in her band 'Uncle G' that they had put a concert together for me called 'Music for Molly' where mummy's band 'Echo' played music for me and that they had managed to raise the money to pay my bill and bring me home forever. I was so grateful and wished I could go and thank and lick everyone individually who had donated money or attended the concert. Thanks to you all and everyone at the vets I was feeling much better and feeling very optimistic for my future.

The next day Mummy and Daddy came to pick me up and take me to my new forever home. Even though Mummy had been coming to see me at the vets every day I was still really frightened about leaving my cage to go with her and my new Daddy. I was still unable to move and so 'auntie' Natalie from the vets had to pick me up to carry me as they were all convinced I was struggling on my legs from the accident or maybe I had seized up, so they carried me to the car where the first discovery was that I was bleeding.... I had come into season!

Once I got to my new home, Daddy carried me out of the car and into a special area he had built for me only that day. He gave me some yummy biscuits and a really tasty meaty chew. There was a really warm kennel and a big blanket and even a radio and on the windowsill, was a get-well card for me sent by some of the local people who generously sent donations to help with my vet bill. It was all very nice but I was eh austed from all the apprehension & worry of going to a strange place so I had a little wonder around and then fell to sleep.

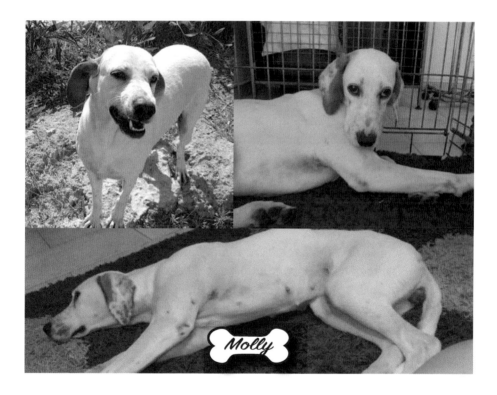

Molly

The nek morning, I was introduced to my new brothers and sister one by one. I was so exi ted my tail did not stop wagging. Mummy and daddy were worried that Lucky my big sister who weighed around 30kg at the time would hurt me so I only had a couple of minutes with her but I loved her and didn't care how big she was I just wanted to be with her. I met my brothers Shammy & Henry who made a fuss but not like Lucky, I know she really liked me and I liked her too. I was sad when mummy and daddy put them back in their area of the garden and all I could think about was getting to see them and to run free. Throughout the morning mummy fed me a delicious breakfast and gave me belly tickles and cuddles but I was still very stiff when either she or daddy touched me as I didn't like humans that much because of what had happened to me in the past. It's hard to trust anyone when you feel like I did.

I kept very quiet and did minimal walking around in my area but once mummy went inside I tried to work out how I would escape as I wanted to be free and away from humans.

I am not sure exactly how it happened as there was a big fence and gate but I focused all my concentration and energy on escaping and before I knew it I was the other side of the gate! At that moment mummy came in to check on me, she realised I was outside the gate and gently called me, but I was frightened that I would get into trouble so I ran like the wind as fast as I could!

Mummy was frantic running after me, mummy and daddy and everyone at the vets had underestimated me, I had even underestimated myself and how fast I could still run. I looked around and mummy was running and calling but that just made me run further, I dashed over a main road and into a field. Mummy must have rung daddy because soon enough they were both in the field chasing after me. Daddy got close and was talking so kindly and quietly to me that I nearly let him grab me, but then I remembered he was human and I was probably going to be in trouble so I ran and ran and ran.

Seven hours came and passed, I remained in and around one particular field as the weeds were so high no-one could see me and when mummy and daddy came through the field it was so hard to navigate and see clearly they would never find me. During the day on a few occasions they spotted me in and around the field, by this time mummy was crying and five other people had joined the search, but more people made me more nervous. At around 7pm mummy came back into the field with 'auntie Natalie' from the vets. She tried to temp me out with treats but I was not going to show my face for anyone I was so frightened!

It started to get dark and I began to get really hungry. Little did I know but mummy and daddy had anticipated this and where waiting for me, camped outside in the garden in the dark. I returned around 10pm as all was quiet. I crept into the purpose-built area daddy had built for me and sure enough there was a yummy dish of food and a big bowl of water. I had not drunk or eaten since early in the morning and I was desperate! Before I knew it the gate had shut behind me, daddy had made a little trap with a rope so he could shut the gate when I arrived so I would not run away again.

Mummy and daddy would not stop hugging me and both of them at the same time! It freaked me out all this human contact at once. They said they had underestimated how well I had recovered and how agile I was. They said they thought based on the day's antics I would be ok to go in with my new brothers and my sister Lucky. I was so excited and so was Lucky, she pounced on me to let me know she is the boss but that is fine, I just want to follow and learn from her. We ran together, played together, ate together, ran around the house together, snuggled on the rug together and all the time my tail did not stop wagging. Mummy and daddy should never have worried... all I wanted was to be with other animals who have my immediate trust, with humans my trust was going to take a little longer

I loved my new brothers and sister as soon as I moved into the main dog area with them. I have found my confidence and now when Shammy, Henry and Lucky jump up for a cuddle or a stroke from mummy and daddy, so do I! Yes, I am licking mummy and daddy's hand and jumping up to them just like my brothers and sister. I have also found my bark and have been showing the others how I too can protect the property and see off any imposters. Lucky has given me the responsibility of being chief watch for rats or mice, I like this job and it proves that I am one of the pack... so I have been practicing my bark to sound strong and scary. I have also been play fighting and my legs are much stronger, in fact to look at me now you would never know I had been run over. I now have my own family, a huge field to run around in twice a day with mummy and daddy and all the other dogs and finally feel like I am safe and that I belong.

Chapter 5

A RIGHT CHARLIE

There were seven of us in my litter, four boys and three girls. We were born on the streets, well under a dustbin actually. Our mother had been on the streets all her life and had been hit by a car on two separate occasions so she limped everywhere she went, not able to use her back legs properly.

Because she was slow and not in the best of health we were left to fend for ourselves from the beginning. Sadly, two of my sisters and one of my brothers didn't make it past a few weeks old through disease and lack of food. At about two months old I knew I had to leave the litter. There was too much competition for food even between by brothers and sister and me. Mum was really weak and couldn't help us. I told her I was leaving; she was very sad and said she was worried she would never see me again. I told her I was going to find food and better shelter and that I would come back for her and my brothers and sister.

I spent weeks wandering the streets, following my nose, fighting both dogs and cats for whatever scraps I could find. I learned about roads and cars and how dangerous they were after a couple of near misses and became aware of people and never missed any opportunity to put on my cutest face and beg for food.

After what must have been a couple of months, I followed my nose back to where I had left my mum and the rest of my litter. I had found better shelter for us all in an open garage not far away. No food yet but I was working on it and I had learned a lot of new skills of how to find food while I had been away on my adventure. I was confident once I got my family somewhere safe I would have no problem sourcing food especially if I took my brothers and sister out hunting with me.

As I approached the bins where we were born I could see my mum laid out in the sun. I started to run towards her, I hadn't realised how much I had missed her and couldn't wait to tell her the good news about our new place to live with lots of room and shade away from the sun. I got in close and snuggled my nose underneath her chin as I had always done from being a pup but she didn't respond so I started gently biting her ears to wake her up but she still didn't move. I thought she was playing a game with me and pretending to be asleep so I tugged on her ears a bit more and ran around her in circles barking loudly for her to wake up as I had good news to tell her.

It took me another few minutes before I realised that she was never going to wake up. She had been so weak after giving birth to us all and I knew her health was bad but never did I think on the day that I left her that it would be the last time I ever saw her. At first I was numb and in shock and I searched around the area calling out for my brothers and sister but couldn't see them anywhere. By this time, I could feel myself getting upset, if only I hadn't left her maybe she would be ok, I could have looked after her and helped her. I got mad with myself, pacing up and down looking at my poor mother and thinking about the tough, horrible life she had been through. I felt so exhausted, disappointed and alone. Eventually I gave in to all my hurt and sadness and curled up in a ball forcing myself underneath my mum's front paw and cried myself to sleep.

That was the moment that made me become tough and fearless. I stayed there with my mum's body, searching around for my brothers and sister for three more days but finally resigned myself to the fact that they were gone and I had to take care of myself. I snuggled under my mum's chin one last time and licked her goodbye before taking off up the road. I knew that I had changed forever and that I needed to be tough and fearless if I was going to survive on my own. I knew I was only small and most dogs and even some cats were bigger than me but what I lacked in size I made up for with my growl and my bark. I feared nothing and no-one!

A few years passed and at that time I had found an area of houses that was proving good for food as the people there all seemed to throw so much away. Of course, there was a lot of competition with other cats and dogs but I had built up a reputation so very few tried to challenge me once I had the food in my mouth. I would also get sympathy food sometimes from some of the residents in the area but no-one ever wanted to take me in as their own. But I didn't care, I had given up on that a long time ago, I could survive, I didn't need anybody anyway!

In my experience not all humans are nice and on several occasions I had encountered some young boys who thought it would be fun to throw things at me or tie things to my tail. I always did my best to avoid them but on this day, they had caught up with me on the corner whilst I was sniffing through the bin. As soon as I saw them I made a run for it but they had longer legs than me and were very fast and before I knew it a big stone hit me on the back of the head. Ouch! I turned and growled at the boys trying to put on my scariest look but they did not seem to fear me at all and continued to throw one stone after another. Just as I was considering leaving the area forever despite its good source of scraps of food a man pulled up in a van. He shouted at the boys to leave me alone in a big booming voice, the boys looked scared and ran off and as they did I couldn't resist putting on my loudest scariest growl and shouting after them. Yeah they were scared now I had backup huh, told you no-one messes with me!

The man in the van opened the passenger door and shouted me to jump in. I learned later that one of the ladies in the street had been having her car cleaned by the man and had told him of a little stray dog who was being bullied and has had his ears chopped off! I didn't know this at the time and couldn't be one hundred percent sure he wouldn't hurt me but, he had got rid of the bullies and humans generally meant food so, without hesitation I jumped in his van.

The first thing he did was make a fuss of me and stroke me, it had been a long time since I had experienced affection from anyone and I lapped it up giving him my cutest puppy dog smile although I was no longer a puppy. He started to pull at my ears gently and when he saw they were fully intact he started to laugh. Sometimes when I am running my ears fold back which is probably what the lady had seen when she thought someone had chopped my ears off. I had been badly treated by many humans and had a challenging life so far but had not experienced cruelty to that level and couldn't even image how horrible that would have been and that there were people out there that would do that.

The man drove for a short while and we arrived at a house with a huge garden. I could hear dogs barking in the garden and I could smell them as well as…….. cats! Lucky for me the man took me straight into the house and gave me some delicious meat. Having lived off other people's left overs all my life I couldn't believe how tasty the meat was and I think the man realised that as he filled my bowl up twice.

Not long afterwards a lady arrived. She made a big fuss of me and said that I was cute and adorable, which obviously, I am! I had just got to thinking how this place would make a perfect forever home for me when I heard the man say that I may belong to someone and they should check me out at the vets and put a notice in the vets and on Facebook for anyone looking for a missing dog. My heart sank, I knew I didn't belong to anyone and having tasted that yummy meat had kind of got to thinking that I might like to belong to a human, especially with a garden this sie and cats to chase.

Charlie

The vets confirmed I was not chipped however, the Facebook appeal did get a response which was a huge surprise to me. A man from a place called Larnaca said he had lost his dog and I looked just like him and that he would like to come and meet me. I started to think It might be to my advantage to be this man's dog or at least try and convince him I was. Anyone who was worried enough about their pet to come all the way from Larnaca must be a nice person and I couldn't be sure what would happen to me if he did not take me home with him.

I spent the morning in the garden cleaning myself ready for the big visit. I could hear the other dogs in the back part of the garden getting excited and barking as the man's car arrived. He stepped out of the car with what I presumed was his son and he walked straight up to me tapping his hand on his thigh and shouting for me to come to him in Greek. I was ready and did exactly what he asked even though he was calling me by a Greek name I had never heard of before. I did my best ever cute look and jumped up and down in front of him, I even threw in a little tail chase to impress. The man patted my head and called me a good boy in Greek (I had picked up quite a lot of Greek on my travels over the years) and then turned to his son and they both shook their heads. Right in that moment I froze, I stopped my cute impression, stopped my tail chasing and sat down on the floor in the garden with my head down, I had failed to make them love me.

The man and his son left and I could hear the man and the woman who's home I was in, talking. I was so sad and disappointed I couldn't even be bothered to get nearer to them to hear what they were saying. Besides I was convinced I knew what they were saying. They were probably saying that as no-one had claimed me and as my ears were perfectly intact they should just take me back to where they found me. They had four dogs already and did not have room for another, especially a small one that might be too small to get along with the big dogs and could possibly be in danger if left alone with them. Clearly they did not know how tough I was and that I had met lots of big dogs in the past and never got scared, in fact most of the time it was the other way around!

I was so busy in my own self pity that I didn't hear the man and woman walking up to me. The lady bent down and stroked me and asked me if I wanted to come and meet my new brothers and sisters. I hadn't moved from on the ground but was letting her stroke me and when she said these words I stayed completely still except for one of my ears that I pricked up to be sure of what I was hearing. The lady continued to stroke me and asked again if I wanted to come and meet my new doggie family. She told me that she was going to be my new mummy and the man who had picked me up in the van was going to be my new daddy. She said that they were going to name me Charlie as I understood English and Greek.

It took me a moment to take in what she was saying and once she had finished speaking I looked from her to the man (my new daddy) and back again to double check that this was really happening. My new daddy smiled and tapped his thigh. "Come on Charlie" he said. Well he didn't have to ask me twice, I was up, not just standing up but up on my back legs springing up and down like a kangaroo with excitement.

I ran around my new mummy's legs and then jumped so high she caught me in her arms. She carried me to the other side of the garden where I had never been before and through the gate I could see four big doggy faces. There was one big black furry dog who was very noisy and yapping at me, another with a big brown nose who was sniffing at me through the gate, a quiet pretty white girl, another white girl dog with a very big head….. and teeth. I started to wonder if I would be in more danger here than out on the streets but then I remembered how fearless I was and gave a little bark to show I was not intimidated but that I wanted to make friends.

This was my chance of a forever home and these chances don't come around very often for dogs like me and I wasn't going to blow it!

Chapter 6

SCOOBY DOOBY DOO

I had a charmed life. I had been with the same family since being a pup. They loved me and fed me and I had my own kennel and a big area to play in.

Some days my mummy and daddy would take me for walks on the beach or for a ride out in the car. I had meat and biscuits every day and treats and toys and Toby their little boy was my best friend, we played together day and night. If we weren't on the field opposite the house playing ball, we were making a den in the garden or playing hide and seek. We were together pretty much all the time except when he went to school, I hated it when he went to school.

Whenever he came home I would run like mad around to the front of the house to jump up and lick him. He would make a big fuss of me calling me a good boy and on most occasions, he would give me a dog treat which he sometimes kept in his pockets for this very purpose. Life just couldn't get any better really, I was so happy.

But then everything changed, it was just little things at first but over time everyone stopped spending time with me and began to ignore me.

First it was Toby; he had made friends with a boy called Tom who lived two streets away and was always out playing with him if he wasn't at school. Whenever he came home I would run like mad around to the front of the house as I had always done to jump up and lick him but he would just tell me to get down or say "Not now".

Then it was my mummy and daddy, they seemed very pre-occupied with things in the house, they were always packing things in boxes and emptying things out of cupboards and wardrobes. I mean I know you must spring clean occasionally but this was getting ridiculous and I wasn't getting any more walks or trips to the beach. In fact, most of the time they didn't even acknowledge me and I was left to just stand in the garden on my own.

Those few weeks were the worst time of my life. I just couldn't figure out what I had done wrong to make everyone so mad at me and not interested in me anymore. I would often gaze through the patio doors that faced into the front room and see them all in the house laughing and joking and I would jump up and scratch on the window to get their attention but they would just shout at me to get down and go to my kennel.

One very hot summers morning they were all up very early and running about the house with yet more boxes when a big lorry came to the house. Two men jumped out and proceeded to take one box after another after another out of the house and load it into the lorry. This went on for hours and Toby had locked me around the back of the garden whilst they were doing this which meant I couldn't see exactly what was going on.

It was nearly getting dark when the lorry finally left and then shortly afterwards daddy came out into the garden with some food and water for me. This was strange as I usually got fed in the mornings but I wasn't going to argue, I was always hungry and gobbled the meat up straight away. Daddy held my face in his hands and said "Now you be a good boy and stay here." Well I wasn't planning on going anywhere except to bed anyway but it was the first bit of attention I had received from anyone in a while so I wagged my tail to let him know I would be good and do what he said.

The next morning came and daddy was late bringing me my food. He would usually bring me it before he went to work. I so looked forward to breakfast time, it was the only time I ever got any human contact these days although it was just daddy putting a bowl down and then walking away. I can remember thinking that he might have a day off work or he might not be well and so I would give him a little extra time to bring it, but I did notice the car wasn't in the drive so maybe he had already gone out and forgot me.

Some time passed and I started to worry about my breakfast as it seemed hours and hours since I had woken up and I was certain that half the day had gone. Then I remembered that daddy gave me some food the night before so maybe he had to go somewhere before breakfast and knew he would not have time this morning and that was why he gave me the food last night. I decided that was definitely it and I would wait until he returned home when I was sure he would remember.

The day dragged on and the summer heat was making me pant heavily and I had drunk nearly all my water in my bowl. I so hoped daddy would be home soon as I was thirsty and hungry now. Soon it was dark and still no daddy or mummy or Toby. I had a good wonder around the garden and I couldn't see them or any sign of them anywhere. I remember daddy had told me stay here and be a good boy and I did not want to let him down so I went back to my kennel and fell into a deep sleep.

The next morning, I woke to the sound of the gate opening. Yipee I thought, they are home. I had missed them all and I wondered if they had missed me and just maybe Toby would let me jump up and lick him and then give me a treat just like he had done in the past. As I came around the corner from the back garden I saw the postman going out of our gate. It must have been him I heard as there was still no car and no mummy, daddy or Toby.

The day went on pretty much the same as the last. I was so hungry and very, very thirsty now as it was so hot. I tried to stay in the shade but even in my kennel it was boiling. I decided to go around to the front of the house to see if I could get a more shaded spot under the tree. I would also be able to see mummy, daddy and Toby when they finally came back.

I walked around to the front and decided to look through the patio door into the house to make sure they weren't in the house. If they were I would scratch on the window to remind them that I needed food and water. More and more they kept forgetting about me and I was getting very upset about it. I stood up on my back legs and peered through the window but my family were not there. As I gazed through the patio door I suddenly realised something very strange. The house was empty! Everything was gone! All the furniture, the plants, the TV, everything! I ran around to the back of the house and tried my best to jump up to see through the kitchen window. It was quite high up and I couldn't climb that high but I could jump to give myself just enough time to catch a glimpse and sure enough the table and chairs, the microwave, the fridge, everything was gone!

I didn't understand what this all meant, daddy had told me to stay here and be a good boy, but what did he mean? How long did I have to stay and wait? It was so hot and I was so thirsty, I didn't know how much longer I could wait for them to return. I went and found shelter under the tree in the front garden and as the hours passed I was more and more hungry and thirsty and lonely. The more I sat and thought about everything the more upset I got until I was overcome with sadness and began to howl loudly crying for my family to come back. Eventually, when I could cry no more I fell asleep.

I awoke as it was getting dark and there was still no sign of anyone but at least it had cooled down and there was a breeze now. Suddenly I heard a squeaking noise, I jumped up to see what it was and noticed the front gate was swinging in the wind. The postman must have not put the catch on properly and now there was a breeze the wind was blowing the gate. I sat and thought for a minute, my mouth was so dry and I was hungry. I know my daddy had said to stay and be a good boy but I couldn't go any longer without water so I got up and waited for the wind to blow the gate open again and ran out into the street. I walked to the field across the road where Toby and I used to play. I was so happy then, I just couldn't understand what had gone wrong or why my family had left me.

At the other side of the field was a house with a big driveway and a swimming pool. There was no gate so I walked quietly down the driveway not wanting to disturb anyone or let them know I was there. I laid my body down on the concrete and hung my head over the side of the pool and drank for what seemed like forever.

After finally quenching my thirst I headed out of the garden and noticed a black bin liner at the end of the driveway. I remember thinking that it must be the bin night. I always knew when it was bin night because a big lorry with flashing lights would come when it was dark. The lights and noise always used to scare me and I would bark at the dustbin men who made such a clattering noise which hurt my big floppy ears. I followed my nose to the black bag, I was pretty sure I could smell food. I ripped open the bag with my teeth and sure enough there was some left-over chicken and potatoes. I never remembered food tasting so good as it did that night, the first time in my life I had had to hunt for my own food.

Totally exhausted and satisfied having now had something to eat and drink I was very sleepy. I wasn't sure what to do as I had never slept anywhere other than in my garden or my kennel but my house was a long way off in the distance and if I went back and slept in my kennel the postman might come in the morning and lock the gate so I couldn't get out again. With this thought in my head I decided to make myself a bed for the night in the long grass in the field where Toby and I used to play.

The nek morning, I awoke early. The first thing I did was run back home to see if mummy, daddy and Toby had returned but just as before there was no-one in sight. With a heavy heart, I set off up the street to the main road wondering where my nek meal was coming from and what sort of horrible, lonely life was now in store for me. I followed the main road for some time and once again the temperature was getting hot and I found myself panting and thirsty. I decided to follow a long gravel driveway which ran off the main road to a house I could see in the distance in the hope that they had a swimming pool where I could get water.

Scooby

As I walked down the drive I heard a car pulling up slowly behind me and a lady got out of the car and bent down to me and said "Hello little fellow, where did you come from?" I was so pleased to see a friendly face and licked her ear to thank her for stopping to talk to me. She scooped me up and put me in her car and drove us the rest of the way down the drive. She carried me out of the car and through some big gates. I could hear lots of dogs barking and I jumped out of her arms and ran across the garden to get away as all the loud barking scared me. The lady laughed and disappeared into her house returning shortly afterwards with a big bowl of meat and biscuits and a big bowl of fresh, ice cold water. I remember thinking to myself that I was in doggy heaven!

After I had finished eating and drinking the lady stroked me and asked me if I belonged to anyone and if I was lost. Of course, I couldn't answer her and explain what had happened and that my family had left me but it was as if she understood as she scooped me up and put me back in the car and took me to see a nice vet.

The vet confirmed that I was tagged and they had found out who my family were. I was so relieved; I had walked for such a long time I would never remember my way back home not even with my super sensitive nose. But this man now knew who I belonged to so the lady could take me back to be re-united with my family. Surely they would be back home by now.

The vet frowned and said to the lady "I am really sorry for this little boy but according to our veterinary nurse who lives on the same street as this dog's family they moved back overseas to their home country three days ago." The lady looked horrified and asked the vet how people could be so cruel. The vet said that they had seen this happen many times when people move back to their home countries and find it too expensive to take their animals with them. He said that many leave their animals but find them a new home first, some leave their animals at the pound and some as is the case with me, just leave their animals all together.

Having heard this the lady gave me a huge hug saying "You poor baby, how could they do this to you?" I couldn't understand it either and I was upset about my family leaving but I was also feeling safe now as I knew this lady would not leave me to walk the streets and go hungry and thirsty again.

She drove me back to her house where a man had now arrived. He was kind too and made a big fuss of me. The lady told the man what the vet had said, she was very emotional whilst telling him my story which made me emotional too so I snuggled into her arms so she knew I understood and how grateful I was that she had saved me. After talking for a while the lady and the man told me that this was going to be my new home and that I would have five brothers and sisters to play with and lots of space to run around.

I was so excited, I did just that, I ran around the swimming pool three times in delight. I was so relieved that they were not taking me to the pound to be locked up with all the other poor doggies that didn't have a home or someone to love them. Having experienced for the first time what it is like to be completely alone and scared I knew I never wanted to feel that way again and was so grateful to have a new loving forever home and family.

Chapter 7

A DROP OF BRANDY

Have you ever been really hungry? I mean starving, and so lacking in nutrition that your rib gage literally shows through your skin? Well that's how I have been all my life for as far back as I can remember.

I was born on the streets and was the only one of a litter of four to survive. My mother died soon after giving birth to us and so began a life of extreme hunger and loneliness. Hunting for food, water and shelter was pretty much all I focused on every day. Some days were better than others and you would get lucky and find scraps in a bin before any other dogs or cats got them. Other days you would have to fight off two or three others to be in with a chance of eating and some days you didn't eat at all. I know how to beg to humans and this is where the most quality food comes from but it is not a reliable or regular source of food and some humans are just downright nasty so there is always the risk of getting hurt when approaching them.

On one occasion, I was walking through a field and heard a very loud bang and then as if by magic a bird fell out of the sky and landed just a few meters away from me. The first thing that came into mind was that there must be a doggy God out there who had sent me a readymade dinner! I pounced on the bird, it was definitely dead and just as I was getting my teeth into it I heard a loud bellowing voice shouting from the distance telling me to get away from the bird. Although I was frightened I was very hungry so I ignored the person shouting and carried on eating. The next thing I remember was hearing a loud bang followed by a sharp pain in my ribs and then falling to the floor. The bangs and the pain kept coming and I didn't know what was happening, all I could think about was how I was in so much pain but I had to try and continue to reach for the bird.

The last loud bang was the most painful of all. One minute I was looking at the dead bird and trying to figure out if I could still reach it and the next minute I felt a sharp shooting pain in my right eye and then everything went black.

I awoke what must have been an hour or so later and couldn't see anything out of my right eye. I looked all around me but the bird had gone and all I could feel was throbbing pain all over me. That was the day I lost my sight in my right eye forever. I had been shot 27 times all over my body by a pellet gun. It took me weeks to recover from the pain and it was so difficult for me to hunt for food or fight off other animals when I was in such a terrible state. These were probably the darkest days of my doggy life so far.

Life got back to normal eventually and I continued to hunt for food and look for shelter every day. Winter came and it was bitterly cold and with my thin malnourished body I felt the drop in temperature even more so.

One day I found myself at a very big road, bigger than I have ever seen, with cars going faster than I had ever seen before. I knew I had to cross the road as there was the possibility that there was food at the other side as it was an area I didn't recognise the smell of..... a new hunting ground. I tried to gage the distance and time between the cars and took three deep breaths and then ran for my life. I could see a car coming at me at a very fast speed and the driver was beeping his horn for me to move out of the way but he didn't slow down. Even with just one eye I could see the immediate danger and I felt the adrenaline pump through my body as I ran as fast I could to the other side of the road with the car narrowly missing me by just a few inches.

After that experience I stopped to catch my breath and take in what had very nearly just happened and as I did a car pulled up behind me with a lady and a man inside who were calling me to come to them. I was frightened and they didn't look like they were offering me any food so I jumped over the barrier at the edge of the road and ran into the nearest field without looking back.

A few days after this I found a shop, a shop where there were lots of people coming in and out all the time. A great place to try and beg for food I thought so I made my way over towards it. I had just reached the front entrance and a lady called out to me but I got scared as she was coming up to me and she didn't have any food in her hand so I ran off. I waited for a few minutes then made my way back towards the shop as I had now spotted someone eating outside which was a good opportunity for me to beg and if I was lucky I might get a scrap or two.

Back at the entrance another lady approached me and she called out softly to me. I wouldn't go to her but didn't run away either. She disappeared and then came back with a bowl of food and some water. I had hit the jackpot this time, a full bowl of food just for me! After eating I gave her a very grateful look and was about to be on my way when she brought over a man to meet me. He spoke to me very softly and started to stroke me, I was so grateful for the food and now some love and kindness that I let him continue. Once he gained my trust he picked me up and put me into the back of the lady from the shops' car, gave me a stroke goodbye and called me a 'good boy' and then off he went.

The lady whose name I now know to be Helen, drove me to see a nice vet who immediately admitted me to his doggy hospital. He said I was so thin and in such bad condition it was unlikely I would have survived many more days especially as this was New Year's Eve and everywhere would be shut for the next twenty four hours or more. I spent several days in the doggy hospital where I was fed to build up my strength and given medicine to help me get strong. These were the best days of my life up to that point. Regular food, uninterrupted sleep, shelter, warmth and love and affection from the staff who were all so very kind to me.

Brandy

A few days later, when I was feeling a lot better and stronger, the man who had lifted me into Helen's car arrived at the doggie hospital with another lady. The vet let me out of the cage and the man picked me up and put me in his car, then he and the lady he was with got in the car and drove me to their home. I didn't really know what was going on but they talked so nice to me and showed me affection so I wasn't frightened at all. The man lifted me out of the car and carried me into   the house. The lady got me a big bowl of food and some water whilst the man disappeared into another room. Regular and tasty food again and warmth in the house, I was so lucky! The man came back with what looked like an old fluffy jumper which he tied around my body to keep me warm. I was still so thin and   my ribs were still showing and the weather was very cold outside so I was very grateful, I had never felt warmth like this before. The man took me outside to walk around the garden and as I approached a big fenced off area I saw six wet noses staring back at me. Even though I was still weak I couldn't stop wagging my tail with excitement as they all seemed very friendly although I didn't want to have to fight off the big white girl or the big fluffy black boy for food!

I sniffed them through the gate and wagged my tail even more. Usually when I saw another dog it meant I needed to fight to survive, I had never really played before but I found myself wanting to play more than anything in the world. Just then the lady came out in the garden with a brand-new lead and a doggy coat for me. She removed the fluffy jumper that I was wearing as a makeshift coat and replaced it with the jacket. It was so warm, I loved it and I licked her hand to say thank you.

I spent the rest of the day in the garden with the man who was building a big fence. He told me that he was going to be my new daddy and the lady was going to be my new mummy. Never in my short, sad doggy life did I think that I would find a loving family like other dogs had that I had seen living in nice gardens with food and love and affection every day. I couldn't believe it!

My new mummy told me that it was fate that I had come to live with them as they were the people who pulled up on the big road a couple of days before and then daddy came to the shop to buy a bottle of Brandy and there I was again. I couldn't believe my life had changed so dramatically over just a few days, I was so happy and I followed my new daddy everywhere he went after that, he is my hero and the one who named me Brandy after the drink he was buying the day he found me.

My life now looks completely different and so does my body. I am so happy and healthy; you wouldn't believe I was the same dog as before. Instead of fear and fighting and starvation and trying to find shelter and warmth, my days are filled with playtime with my brother and sister doggies, sunbathing, eating, playing with balls and rocks on the land with mummy and daddy and having a snooze whenever I fancy. I really am one very lucky boy.

Chapter 8

HUNGRY LIKE THE WOLFIE

I am a rare breed, not often found in Cyprus due to the climate. This made me even more sought after as a puppy and it wasn't long before a man came to see our litter and took a liking to me over and above my two brothers as I was the only girl. I was very young, only a few weeks old and I was scared to be separated from my mother especially as I didn't even get a chance to say goodbye. I was put in a cage on the back of a pick up truck and we drove for what seemed like hours until finally we arrived at a big house with big iron gates.

The man lifted me out of the truck and took me straight to a big metal garage with a concrete floor. There was a bowl with some biscuits and a bowl with water and a big metal chain. He pulled out a collar which he soon realised was far too big for me and so he disappeared into the house and came back shortly afterwards with some big scissors. The scissors were nearly as big as me and as he approached me with them I feared for my life.

He cut off quite a bit of the length of the collar and then used the scissors to bore an extra hole so that the collar would fit tight enough around my neck. He then attached the big heavy chain to my collar and without saying a word he stood up and disappeared into the house. I had never been alone before, I had always been with my mother and brothers. The concrete floor was so uncomfortable to lay on and I longed to snuggle up to my mothers breast as I had done so many times before.

For the rest of the day I was left totally alone. There were lots of strange noises I had never heard before and lots of strange smells, I felt so frightened. The chain the man had attached to my collar was so thick and heavy I could barely move but I knew I needed to move away from the front of the garage to stay out of the direct sunlight so using all my strength I slowly moved right to the back of the garage dragging the huge chain behind me. Exhausted, I curled up in the back corner making myself small enough so as not to be seen from the outside. I tried to reassure myself that from this angle I could see anyone or anything coming my way but I wasn't sure what I was intending to do about it if they did!

From that day on this was my life. I never went out for walks, I never went in the house and the man would come just once a day to bring me food and water. He never really spoke to me and never really made a fuss of me. We had no physical contact at all. This wasn't a life, it wasn't even an existence, it was pure misery.

Every day I was growing bigger and getting more curious about the world outside. I had discovered on one of my recent investigations that the heavy chain attached to my collar was very short, giving me just enough length to go to the toilet outside or to lay immediately at the front entrance to the garage. It didn't reach to the grass or the flower bed, in fact it didn't reach to anything other than what I already knew, a concrete floor and a metal, corrugated garage.

Spending all this time alone with no stimulation or exercise of any kind left me with only my imagination and my dreams of a life I would much prefer. I would close my eyes and imagine I had broke free from the chain and that I was running through the field across the road, jumping through the grass and investigating a million different smells that I would come across along the way. I dreamed of having playmates that I could chase around just like I had done as a baby with my brothers. Most of all I dreamed of having a purpose because sitting there every day alone, well where was the purpose in that?

Life went on like this for a while, I was so unhappy and alone. Why didn't the man talk to me or stroke me or take me out for walks? Once when he had brought my food I tried to lick his hand to have some physical contact with him, to show him that I was grateful for my food and maybe get him to love me but he just brushed me aside saying "Get off!" I never tried again after that.

One day whilst I was staring out at the field across the road daydreaming about a better life, a lady and her dog walked past. Her dog spotted me in the doorway to my kennel and tried to run into our garden towards me, he was barking really loudly, I think he wanted to play and so did I. My tail started wagging faster than ever before and I ran out of my garage towards him forgetting all about the chain on my neck but was soon reminded when it pulled hard and stopped me in my tracks as I came to the end of its length.

But the stupid chain wasn't going to stop me so I began to howl at the top of my voice. I discovered that I was really good at this although the few times I had practiced it the man had opened the window from the house and shouted at me really loudly and scarily so I had soon learned to be quiet.

The dog's owner was trying to pull him back but her dog was really determined and broke free from her grip on his lead. By this time I was howling louder than ever with anticipation and as the dog reached me we both jumped around sniffing at each other with excitement.

The lady owner came running up to us then stopped, catching her breath before she spoke. "Scamp come back here what's got into you?" Scamp wasn't paying any attention he was too busy licking my face and I loved it so I licked him right back. Then the lady saw me and bent down to stroke me. I don't ever remember being stroked before that it felt so nice. Suddenly the man pulled onto the drive with his truck. His face was really angry and I pulled away from the lady's arm and ran back into my garage.

"What do you think you are doing?" he bellowed at the lady. "I am so sorry, my dog pulled free and came running into your garden to meet your dog, I think they like each other." The man stood and looked at the woman and Scamp for a second and then said "Dogs don't have feelings, they don't like things, they just are. Now get off my land!"

The lady looked horrified, she quickly grabbed Scamp's lead and ran back up the driveway towards the main road. I peered out of my garage to watch them leave and although he was being dragged pretty fast, Scamp managed to turn his head one more time and give out a big bark with a promise that we would see each other again. The man took one disgusted look at me then turned and walked up to the house.

For the next few days all I could think about was Scamp and if today would be the day he and his lady owner passed by again but they never did. At night I would howl with sadness wanting to be with my only friend in the world. I just wanted someone to play with, I so hated being on my own all the time.

One night I was particularly sad and started howling. It was very dark until I saw the headlights of the man's truck pull up on the driveway. As he got out of the truck I could see him wobbling around. He started to walk up to my garage which was strange as he never came with food or water late at night. As he approached me he stumbled and just managed to stop himself from falling by grabbing hold of the garage wall. He smelt funny, different to his normal smell and he was speaking funny, slurring his words.

"So you want to go and play with your friend do you? Howling day and night you are nothing but a nuisance, I don't know why I bother. Think you've got it bad do you? Think you could manage better without me? Well go on then off you go you good for nothing waste of space." I didn't really understand what was going on, he was acting so strangely, I knew he was mad with me but I couldn't understand why.

He bent down and walked into my garage, I ran right to the back and cowered, I was really scared now. "I said Go!" he shouted and with that he grabbed my chain and pulled me by the neck to him. I screamed in fear and pain, it really hurt. He gave the chain one final tug towards him so I was face to face with him and then with a big yank pulled the chain free of my collar. " Now go!" he shouted and smacked me on my back so hard I nearly jumped out of my skin. Without thinking I ran straight passed him over the main road and into the field. I ran until I couldn't run any more not even stopping to look back because the one thing I knew in my mind for sure is that I was never going back.

That night I slept down a dark alley, I was so scared the man would come looking for me and take me back to my doggy prison.

The next morning when I awoke I was filled with optimism. I was free. I put my nose to the ground and for the first time in my short doggy life I sniffed the grass. I leapt around in the field finally living my dream of freedom taking in every noise, sight and smell for the first time.

Suddenly it occurred to me, now I was free I could go and find Scamp and we could run and play together. Finally I would have a playmate. I darted to the other side of the field and came to a big road wondering how I was ever going to find Scamp when I didn't have a clue where he lived. As I had never been out of my garage I didn't really know about roads or cars so was given a big shock when I started to hear lots of loud beeping behind me, no-one had told me you shouldn't walk down the middle of a road. I was frightened and confused so I shot from one side of the road to the other narrowly being missed by a car and a truck. Just then a man came walking into the middle of the road and picked me up. At first I was scared but then he started to talk to me in nice voice telling me that roads are very dangerous and that I could have been killed. He lifted me up into his big van and we drove for a short while before arriving at his home. He made up a bed for me on the floor and gave me the most delicious meal I had ever eaten which I now know as pork chop. Mmm I really like pork chop!

The nek day after having had what was probably the best sleep of my life, I woke up to that delicious pork smell again but this time the man told me it was called bacon. Mmm I really like bacon. He told me he couldn't keep me because his garden was too small and he was out at work all day but he knew of a place where there was lots of land for me to run around on and lots of other doggies to play with. This sounded like the life I had dreamt of every day chained up in the garage and so I became very exi ted and ran around his coffee table before jumping up on his knee and licking his face with gratitude.

Later that day we arrived at my new home where there was a man and a lady and lots and lots of other dogs, I couldn't wait to meet them all. The lady and the man made a big fuss of me and gave me a doggy treat. I had never had one of these before, it was so delicious I ate it in one go.

Over the nek few days I got to know my new mummy and daddy better. They were so loving towards me and they played with me and gave me hugs all the time. I loved my new life and the first time I met all of the other seven dogs that were my new brothers and sisters I howled so loudly I think they must have heard me in the next village. My new daddy told me I howled just like a wolf and so they decided to call me Wolfie!

The nice man that had found me (who I will be forever grateful to) and my new daddy built a big fence on the land so I had a big area of my own to play in with lots of grass. I love having my own big kennel with my own sofa in it and I love that I am free to roam on the land whenever I choose but my favourite thing by far and the thing I look forward to the most every day is when daddy and mummy come down on the land with all the other dogs and we get to run and play together.

Sometimes I sit and think about my old life and how lonely and sad I was. All I had ever wanted was some affection, someone to play with and a purpose in life. Now I guard the house and howl if I hear strange noises that might be intruders, my purpose is to protect my family. I get cuddles and so much affection every day, delicious food and treats and now instead of having one playmate I have got seven. I am such a lucky girl and all my doggy dreams really did come true.

Chapter 9

READY FREDDIE

From the moment I met her I loved my human mummy. I was only a pup at the time and the minute we saw each other I knew she would pick me. She cast her eyes over my four brothers and sisters and then spotted me in the corner. I was really quiet compared to the rest of them who were jumping up and down in front of each other doing tricks trying to impress her. But I could tell that wasn't what she was looking for, she wanted someone to cuddle up to at night, a companion who understood her and I knew right then that it would be me.

For the next few months we did everything together. She lived alone and was quiet like me with few friends but a full life none the less. We went on walks twice a day, ate dinner together and cuddled up together at the end of every night on the sofa watching romantic comedies. Bridget Jones was her favourite!

Although we were great companions and had lots of fun together I could tell with my doggy instinct that she was lonely and wanted a human companion as well as having me. At first I was a bit sad about this and a little jealous as I was so happy having her all to myself and being at the centre of her life and everything she did. But, I loved her so much that I knew deep down it was only fair that she should find true happiness and I hoped that one day I would find that special lady doggie too.

We had been together for over a year when she met him. We were on one of our regular walks on the doggie beach and I was splashing around all over the place in the water showing off to mummy like I always did. As I turned to make sure I had her full attention whilst I did my usual tail splash I saw her talking to a man. They were pretty close and I could see their body language was intense! After a minute, she turned around to check where I was and called me to come to her. I had no problem with this and wanted to see this man for myself, only a true gentleman would be good enough for her and a true dog lover.....although he didn't have a dog with him.

I ran up to her and positioned myself right by her side so my head was touching her legs. The man bent down and stroked me and said what a handsome boy I was. I was happy with this and wagged my tail in approval. From then on he came over to the house all the time and we went from a two to a three. He seemed to understand that I was very protective of mummy and so I needed to sit between them on the sofa when he came round but it did mean that I was no longer allowed to sleep on the bed with mummy when he stayed over. At first I was very upset about this but he was kind to me and gently placed me in a really snug doggie bed still in her bedroom so in the end I gave into this for the sake of my mummy as I was still in the same room and could still look after her.

After a few months things started to change and mummy's new man moved in with us. He started to tell mummy that I was spoilt and that she needed to be more firm with me and a dog should know it's place and should not rule the home. I didn't really understand what he was talking about until the week mummy had to go away for work and I was left alone with him. It was like his personality had totally changed, like he was a different person all together to how he was in front of mummy. At night I wasn't allowed in the bedroom at all and he put my bed in the kitchen which was really cold and damp now it was winter. The first night mummy was gone and he did this I cried and cried and cried to be let in but after about 10 minutes the door opened and he grabbed me really roughly by my neck and threw me into my dog bed. I went flying across the room as I was only little and banged my head on the kitchen cupboard as I fell. I yelped in pain but he didn't care he just wagged his finger at me shouting in a really scary voice "Shut up and stay there or I'll give you something to cry for!"

For most of the night I remained quiet whimpering in the corner, my head throbbed with pain and I couldn't understand what I had done to make him so angry with me. After a while I started to scratch at the door, I thought if I tried hard enough and long enough I would be able to create a hole so I could get through and go and lay on the sofa in the warm. It was hard work, but I was so cold in the kitchen and so determined to get back into the living room that I made quite a lot of progress and although I didn't quite finish the hole I knew I was getting close to the centre and one more night at it would probably break me through to the other side.

The next morning, I awoke to a sharp pain in my neck. I didn't understand what was going on at first as I had been working on the door most of the night and had been exhausted by the time I had finally got to bed. I soon came round though as my body tensed up in shock from hitting the concrete outside at full speed, followed closely by my dog bed and my bowl. "Get out and stay out you useless dog" he shouted at the top of his voice.

It seems scratching at the door and my plan to break through to the living room had not helped the situation and I now had severe pain in my back and scratches across my right paw where I had attempted to break my landing. I tried to lick the scratches on my paw to clean them but it really stung and my back throbbed so bending over to tend to myself just made things worse. I was in a mess and couldn't understand how my life could have been so great one day and then so horrific the next.

It was the longest week of my entire doggy life waiting for mummy to come back. He didn't play with me or cuddle me and there were no walks anywhere. He just left me out in the cold in the garden every day whilst he was at work, whereas in the past I had always been allowed to stay at home in the house and watch TV or listen to the radio. I had no treats and on two days he forgot to feed me at all. I have never felt so sad and alone but knew that once mummy came back everything would be back to normal and she would see how cruel he had been to me and ask him to leave.

Eventually mummy returned and I couldn't wait to see her. I heard her car pull up and her voice as she came through the front door. I sat wagging my tail as hard as I could waiting for her to come to the back door and out in the garden to see me but instead I just heard shouting mainly from him. The shouting went on for a while and then I heard a crash and mummy crying. I started to bark as loud as I could, I had to let someone know what was happening so they could come and rescue me and now mummy also. A minute later he was out the door and in the garden coming towards me with a sweeping brush and I ran into the corner cowering away from him. All this time mummy was shouting at him "Leave him, he is just a dog it's not his fault, it's me you are mad at, don't hurt him." As he came closer to me with the sweeping brush I saw mummy run up behind him and grab him to try and distract him from hitting me. I was growling at him and trying to warn him off but inside I was petrified of what he was about to do. As he felt mummy's arms on him he turned around quickly and without intentionally doing it the sweeping brush hit mummy smack on the head and she yelled in pain. At this point he stopped in his tracks and realised what he had done. He fell to the floor where mummy was now crouched down holding her head shouting with tears in his eyes that he was sorry and he hadn't meant to hurt her and that he loved her and wanted to be with her.

I didn't believe a word of it and wanted to go and comfort mummy as she had only got hurt protecting me. I approached slowly and could see the tears streaming down mummy's face whilst he held her tight whispering in her ear. As I grew closer he glanced at me and then looked back at mummy saying "You know what we must do, don't you, if you want us to stay together?" Mummy nodded, the tears still streaming down her face more than ever as she looked over to me and he walked back into the house.

Finally, I was alone with my mummy and I gently licked away the tears from her face and cuddled into her trying to comfort her and reassure her that things would be ok once we were back to how it was, just the two of us. She bent her head down to mine and kissed me on my nose, still very upset, and then she told me that the man had discovered he was allergic to dogs and that having me was making him really ill and that he couldn't possibly be with her or live with her whilst I was under the same roof. She kept saying how sorry she was but that the man was going to find me a good home with children to play with and a loving family who would take me for walks just as she had done. But I didn't want children or a new family, I wanted my mummy. I couldn't understand it, surely mummy was going to choose me over him, after all I was with her first and he had been nasty to both of us. I wanted her to be happy, that is what I have always wanted for her but surely she could never be happy with him now he had shown this side of himself. I snuggled into her licking her tears away once more, she squeezed me tight one last time and then turned away sobbing loudly as she ran into the house.

I just stood frozen in disbelief at what had just happened. I felt sure that given some time to calm down she would come to her senses so when the back door opened shortly afterwards I ran straight towards it thinking it would be her coming to tell me she had changed her mind and he was going, not me. My thoughts were soon interrupted when I saw him with a lead in his hand so I ran and cowered at the back of the garden. He came stomping towards me and picked up my bowl and bed on the way. I remained totally still not wanting to do anything to annoy him or make him mad and without a word he clipped the lead onto my collar and gave me a tug to walk with him out of the garden to the car. I don't know whether it was pure stubbornness or fear but I fixed my paws firmly to the ground and wouldn't move. This didn't stop him or phase him whatsoever, he just pulled even harder and dragged me across the garden burning the bottom of my paws as they scraped against the ground. He picked me up and literally threw me into the back of the car, all the time not saying a word.

I sat with tears in my eyes in the boot of the car looking to see my mummy and waiting for her to come and rescue me. I thought I saw her peering through the window of the house but as soon as I caught sight of her the curtains twitched and she was gone. I closed my eyes hoping that when I opened them again it would all be a bad dream, but when I did open them I was still in the boot of the car and we had pulled up into an industrial area. The boot door opened and his arm appeared inside grabbing onto my lead, he walked me firmly across a gravelled area and up to a netted gate with a big sign hanging from the front. Of course I couldn't read the sign so I had no idea where we were. Was this the entrance gate to my new home with the nice family with children mummy had promised me?

He grabbed my lead and tied it tight to the gate so I couldn't move more than 2 centimetres away, there wasn't even enough slack on the lead for me to lay down. He left me there, went back to the boot and took my bed and bowl out of the back of the car and threw them at me, my bowl narrowly missed my nose and landed just a few centimetres away. With that he got back in the car and sped off into the distance. It was getting dark now and I could hear lots of dogs barking but there wasn't enough slack on my lead to investigate where I was or for me to get to my bowl although there wouldn't be much point as there was nothing in it. I sat feeling more confused, frightened and alone than I have ever felt in my life. It was cold and I was hungry and to make matters worse there were big flashes of light in the sky and big bangs that followed afterwards which I soon learned meant torrential rain was coming. Within ten minutes the heavens opened and there was a huge storm over me. I couldn't run for shelter; I couldn't even curl up in a ball to keep warm and protect myself as my lead was tied too tightly to the gate. I spent the whole night sat getting drenched from the excessively heavy rain and petrified of the loud banging sounds and flashing lights. This was most definitely the longest night of my life.

By the morning I was frozen half to death and wet through. I was so hungry and thirsty that my mouth had gone completely dry and my head was pounding from being exposed to the heavy rain. To be honest I am surprised I survived the night especially as all I could think about was how my mummy didn't love me anymore and that I would never be happy again so I might as well drown in the rain as no-one would even notice I had gone. Just then my ears pricked up at the sound of a car pulling in onto the gravel. A lady I had never seen before got out of the car and spotted me straight away. She came straight over to me and saw that I was shaking and wet through and quickly undid my lead and pulled me into her arms. She was so warm and was wearing a big fluffy jumper that I snuggled right into. "You poor thing" she cried as she unlocked the gate that I had been tied to. Keeping me close to her chest at all times she led me into a room where there was a shower and some towels. She ran some water in the shower and kept feeling it with her hands, just until it warmed up, then stood me gently in the shower and filled her hands with something sweet smelling and soapy. She began to rub it into my belly as the warm soothing water fell on me. She was so calm and her words were so soothing and I was so grateful of her help and of the warm water now falling on my back.

I felt so much better after my shower and wondered if this was going to be my new mummy as I really liked her. She dried me off and then carried me through an area where there were lots and lots of dogs. As soon as they all saw me they barked loudly and I was a bit scared but luckily they were all in cages so they couldn't get near me and I had buried my head into her chest to hide myself.

At the end of the row of barking dogs we stopped and she opened a cage door and put me down on the floor. Latching the gate, she then disappeared and came back a few minutes later with my bed and my bowl that he had thrown at me before leaving me to drown in the rain. I shuddered at the memory of what had happened the night before and felt sure today would be a better day. She came back in and put my bowl and my bed down then she lifted me up into my bed, gave me a stroke and a pat on the head, locked the gate and then disappeared.

I didn't know what to make of it where I was. Was this my new mummy and this cage my new home? I wasn't sure how happy I was about being here with all these other dogs, some were really, really loud and never stopped barking. I had a sniff around my cage and came face to face with a big bushy dog with big droopy eyes. He yapped loudly at me, I think he wanted to play but after the night I had just had I was too tired to do anything but curl up in my bed and fall asleep. I nuzzled my head right down so I could take in the smell of my mummy's scent which still lingered on my bed cover and drifted off to sleep.

I spent a few weeks at the dog pound with all the other dogs not knowing what twists and turns the future still held for me. The ladies and men at the dog pound where I lived were really nice but it was really crammed here and every dog was fighting for food and attention especially as new dogs arrived every day yet not so many were lucky enough to be picked to go and live in a forever home. Most of the dogs in the pound had never had a mummy or daddy or a forever home so I did feel lucky that once I had been happy and never wanted for food or love unlike many of the others. But having had that life and love all I could think of was having it again. Whenever someone came to look to select a dog for a forever home all the other dogs barked and jumped around trying to impress the visitors whereas I was quiet and kept in my bed as I didn't think anyone would want me ever again. I was also really afraid of men, especially ones with deep scary voices and as many of the visitors were families with men I didn't want them to choose me, I had already seen what a man could do and I never wanted to be in that position again.

This is where the big surprise came as one day when several visitors came looking for dogs to give a forever home to and whilst I was in my bed, in my cage not really paying attention I heard a rattle at my cage. I jumped up and looked around and there was a man and a lady staring at me. The next thing I knew one of the ladies from the dog pound was opening my gate and the lady and man came to stroke me. I froze immediately especially as there was a man so close but it did not seem to bother them and the man said that he would have me. I didn't know what to think, I wasn't happy at the pound but I was much more scared of going somewhere with a man I didn't know. Luckily the lady that was with him gave me kisses and cuddles and reassured me that everything was going to be alright.

We arrived at the man's house shortly afterwards and despite the fact that he had a very quiet gentle voice and had put some yummy food out for me I ran straight behind the settee and was scared to come out. When the man went to bed later on that day I slowly crept out from behind the sofa and ate my food and had a good sniff around. The house smelt of another dog but I couldn't work it out as I hadn't seen another dog anywhere but my nose had never let me down before and I vowed to investigate this more the next day.

The next morning came and my new daddy got out a lead and came over to me behind the sofa to encourage me to come out. The lady had left once she had brought me to the man's house the night before and I was still scared to be alone with him even though he did talk really softly to me. I refused to come out, even though I really needed the toilet and could do with a walk and so I stubbornly stayed put despite his many attempts to lure me out with doggy treats.

Not long after that the lady who had come with him to the pound the day before arrived and I soon worked out the mystery of the other dog. There stood before me was a big brown fluffy dog with a black wet nose and a really kind face. Now this was worth coming out from behind the sofa for. We had a good sniff around each other and we even shared my bowl of food, I liked him immediately and hoped he would be staying.

The man sat not too far away from us and in a soft voice told me that he was going to call me Freddie because my new doggie friend was called Barney and it reminded him of the two best friends from the programme The Flintstones. Well I had no idea what he was talking about but I did like the bit about the two best friends and I hoped that Barney and I could be best friends just like them. My new daddy tried to coax me again to put my lead on so he could take me out for a walk but I was still really scared and wouldn't go near the door. I hated being locked behind doors since that horrible day my mummy had left me with the nasty man. But then Barney's mummy put his lead on him and opened the door and with that I let daddy grab my lead and we all went out for a walk together. Me and Barney loved it. We jumped around in the grass playing and chasing each other's tails, we had so much fun and I didn't want him ever to go home but eventually he went back home with his mummy and I was left alone with my new daddy once more.

After what had happened during that day I felt a little more calm with my new daddy and so I decided to lay on the sofa and see what would happen. To my surprise he didn't shout at me like the nasty man had in the past but he cuddled up to me and we watched a film together until the early hours of the morning just like me and my mummy used to do.

Over the next few weeks things just got better and better with me and my new daddy. We went for walks together and with Barney sometimes when he and his mummy came to visit. Daddy took me everywhere to meet all his friends, we even went shopping together. Every night after our walk daddy and me would sit on the sofa and watch TV or listen to nice music that was just like me and daddy, quiet and chilled. He even let me sleep on his bed with him, that is once I had mastered how to get up the stairs on my own. Living in a ground floor flat with my previous mummy and then living at the pound meant I had never exp e-rienced stairs before but I soon learned knowing there was a cosy bed and a warm daddy waiting for me. Life was finally good again.

Freddie

One day a few weeks later I noticed that daddy was a bit slow and wasn't able to take me out for my morning walk so I was a little worried about him. He told me he had to go out but he would be back soon and left me a yummy bowl of meat and biscuits and some water. I patiently waited for him but he was gone a long time and when the door did finally open it was Barney's mum and another lady I had met before that was one of daddy's other friends. They gave me a big fuss and then took me to the other lady's house with my bed and my bowl.
I wondered what was going on and where daddy was but I liked the lady and was happy to stay with her because she spoilt me and gave me lots of cuddles and treats.

That night when Barney and his mummy had gone a man came through the door. I was scared so I cuddled up to the legs of the lady. She told me not to be afraid and that this man was one of daddy's other friends and that they were going to look after me for a while because my daddy was very ill and in hospital.

I wasn't too sure about the man but I kept my distance and cuddled up to the lady on the sofa. A few days passed and I really liked being with the lady but the man had a deep voice and was scary. I know he didn't do anything to me, in fact all he tried to do was be nice to me but I just couldn't trust a man with a deep voice to come between me and a lady again!

After about a week my daddy came out of hospital. He was still very poorly so we didn't go back home, instead he came to live with me the lady and the man with the deep voice. It was great having my daddy back but he was very weak and tired most of the time so we mainly just cuddled up on the sofa or the bed together and it was the lady who took me for walks and fed me. There were lots of other dogs at this house and I could see them through the window, so if daddy was tired and fell asleep I would go and peer through the window at them. I really liked the look of one of the little dogs that looked like me, his name was Scooby. I wanted to play but I had to protect my daddy so I stayed by his side ready to growl at the man when he came in from work just in case he wanted to get too close to my daddy or the lady.

As the weeks went on the man really tried to be my friend but I just couldn't get over my memories of the past and how frightened I had been so I kept my distance and my growl. My daddy was still really ill and he told me he had to go to England to get better and that he might not see me for a very long time. He said he wanted me to be a good boy and stay with the lady and the man who would be my new mummy and daddy and that he would come and visit me as soon as he was feeling better. I wasn't sure what to think of this. I was going to really miss my daddy although of course I wanted him to get better but I just wasn't sure about staying in the house alone with the man with the deep voice or about the fact he was going to be my new daddy.

I licked my daddy goodbye and hoped he would feel better soon, I was really going to miss him but now I didn't have to guard him I could go and play with the other dogs. I wouldn't let my new daddy near me at first but he did open the door and bring Scooby one of the other dogs to play with me. We were the same size and sniffed each other for a while before running faster and faster around the garden.

Having tasted life outside with Scooby I didn't want to be alone in the house on my own anymore and I longed to be with the others and play with them. It was then that my new mummy said she was going to introduce me to another one of the dogs, a girl dog that lived in another part of the garden who didn't want to be alone any more. I was a bit scared at first as I had not seen the girl dog before and I wanted to make sure I looked my best so I cleaned myself up to make a good first impression. My new mummy took me to a massive area of land with a big warm snug house in the middle. She unclipped my lead and I started to run and sniff all the grass when all of a sudden this big white fluffy vision came towards me. It was love at first sight. We sniffed each other, ran around the land together and then disappeared into the big dog house on the land to cuddle up together. Her fur was so warm and fluffy and I was in heaven.

From that day on my life changed forever. I now have a lady doggy in my life, her name is Wolfie. I have my new mummy and daddy and they come down onto the land to play with us every day and I am even growling less at my new daddy as he spoils me and Wolfie and gives us extra food when my other seven brothers and sister dogs aren't looking.

We get to run and play on the land every day, all nine of us together, and sometimes my friend Barney calls around to play. But my favourite time of day is when I am snuggled up with my white fluffy queen. Life doesn't get much better than this!

ABOUT THE AUTHOR

NATALIE REED

Natalie Reed moved to Cyprus with her husband Mark and their son Ashley in 2008 from the UK for a slower pace of life and the cultural experience and fabulous weather Cyprus has to offer.

Natalie is the owner of The Daxi Group who produce a free monthly lifestyle magazine for the English reading and speaking community in South East Cyprus. The Daxi Group also produce a free annual tourist guide which compliments their two tourist information centers. The Daxi Group also host a biennial awards ceremony to recognize the achievements of local businesses, charities and individuals in South East Cyprus.

For seven years Natalie was the lead vocalist in a Cyprus based band called Echo, she now hosts a weekly radio show online called 'The Nuts' on www.ex-patradio.com. as well as making the odd guest vocalist appearance at charity and community events.

www.cyprusstrays.com

Printed in Great Britain
by Amazon